The Pilgrims

Other books in the Daily Life series:

The American Colonies
The American Revolution
Ancient Egypt
Ancient Greece
Apache Warriors
A Cowboy in the Wild West
The Gold Rush
A Medieval Castle
The Oregon Trail
Pirates
A Plains Indian Village

The Pilgrims

Melanie Ann Apel

THOMSON
GALE

San Diego • Detroit • New York • San Francisco • Cleveland
New Haven, Conn. • Waterville, Maine • London • Munich

For more information, contact
KidHaven Press
27500 Drake Rd.
Farmington Hills, MI 48331-3535
Or you can visit our Internet site at http://www.gale.com

LIBRARY OF CONGRESS CATALOGING-IN-PUBLICATION DATA

Apel, Melanie Ann.
The pilgrims / by Melanie Ann Apel.
p. cm.—(Daily life)
Summary: Portrays life aboard the Mayflower and in Massachusetts as the Pilgrims worked, prayed, studied, and lived together in a place that offered religious freedom and land of their own..
Includes bibliographical references.
ISBN 0-7377-0993-6 (hardback : alk. paper)
1. Pilgrims (New Plymouth Colony)—Juvenile literature. 2. Massachusetts—Social life and customs—To 1775—Juvenile literature. 3. Massachusetts—History—New Plymouth, 1620–1691—Juvenile literature. [1. Pilgrims (New Plymouth Colony) 2. Massachusetts—History—New Plymouth, 1620–1691.]
I. Title. II. Series.
F68 .A63 2003
974.4'8202—dc21

2002012172

Printed in China

Contents

Coming to America on the *Mayflower*

Almost four hundred years ago the Pilgrims traveled from England to America to improve their lives. In the year 1620, their trip across the Atlantic Ocean from England to America took sixty-six days. More than one hundred people crowded onto the *Mayflower*. At least thirty of the passengers were children and young people. The Pilgrims hoped to live in a place where they would have land of their own and religious freedom. In England they did not have either of these.

Leaving England

King Henry VIII ruled England in the 1600s. He was also the head of the Church of England. Everyone was expected, and even required, to belong to the Church of England. But the Puritans wanted to leave the Church of England and start their own church in a new land. They booked passage aboard a ship called the *Mayflower*. Others, including a barrelmaker, a soldier, and fourteen **indentured servants** traveled to America in search of a new home.

How the Pilgrims Reached America

In September 1620 the Pilgrims boarded the *Mayflower* to set sail from Plymouth, England. William Bradford, one of the passengers, later wrote that the Pilgrims were unhappy to leave England behind. But the promise of religious freedom and land of their own consoled them.

The *Mayflower* is tossed along the Atlantic Ocean on its way to America in 1620.

And so the Pilgrims embarked on their journey. Because the *Mayflower* was a merchant ship, it was built to carry few people and a lot of cargo, such as cloth and barrels of wine. There were no private cabins and no comfortable beds. The Pilgrims chose spots for themselves between the decks. Each family had only a few feet of space to call its own. Some of the Pilgrims paid the ship's carpenter to build crude double- or triple-tier bunk beds from planks of wood. Others slept in hammocks. The Pilgrims kept many of their belongings, such as their pots for cooking and their clothes, with them. The rest of their things were stored in the **hold**. There was no special place for changing clothes or washing. Those who wished to have any privacy at all for their family created a sort of cabin by hanging canvas around their bunk beds or hammocks. To pass the time on the voyage, the children played together and adults completed chores and made food.

An Uncomfortable Voyage

The Pilgrims' voyage took place in the fall. It was cold and damp. The weather was often stormy. This was a hard time for the passengers aboard the *Mayflower*. Many spent time lying on their bunks feeling seasick. Others lived in fear of drowning. The ship had many leaks, and water often poured in. One passenger nearly drowned when he fell overboard.

At the beginning of the voyage, the Pilgrims had a variety of foods to eat: salted meat and fish, peas, beans, beer, and hard cheese. These were the kinds of foods they were used to eating in England in the winter and early spring. It was not long before their fresh food started to

Pilgrims gather on the *Mayflower* and express their joy in reaching America safely.

run out, though. Then all they had to eat was hard bread, a few onions, some lemon juice, beer, and dried meat, which was green with mold.

The Mayflower Compact

The Pilgrims and the rest of the people aboard the *Mayflower* sometimes fought. As they got closer to America the men came up with a set of rules to follow in the New World. Landing in the New World without a set of laws to follow could have led to some serious problems.

Pilgrim leaders sign the Mayflower Compact. The document contained the plan of their new government.

Before the *Mayflower* docked in Plymouth, Massachusetts, some of the Pilgrims had an idea. With the help of fellow Pilgrim William Brewster, who is believed to have done the writing, they worked on creating a plan for a government for their new land. They called their plan the Mayflower Compact. All the men on board the *Mayflower* signed it. Everyone in their community would have to follow the laws in the Mayflower Compact. One of the agreements was that John Carver, who was already their governor, would remain governor for one more year. John

Carver was also the first person to step forward and sign the Mayflower Compact. The Pilgrims also agreed that their society would guarantee equal justice for all and that the men would work together to make decisions.

The Mayflower Compact became the constitution of Plymouth Colony. It was the first document of America's

Mayflower passengers row toward their new home of Plymouth.

system of democracy, or majority rule. It established "government of the people, by the people, for the people." In fact, even today it is still considered one of the most important documents in American history.

The Tiniest Passengers

Despite the stormy weather, the *Mayflower* made its voyage from England to the New World in just over two months. Only one person died before the ship reached America. By chance, though, the *Mayflower* still arrived in America with the same number of passengers as it had set sail with. A baby named Oceanus Hopkins was born during the long voyage. And just as the ship was docking,

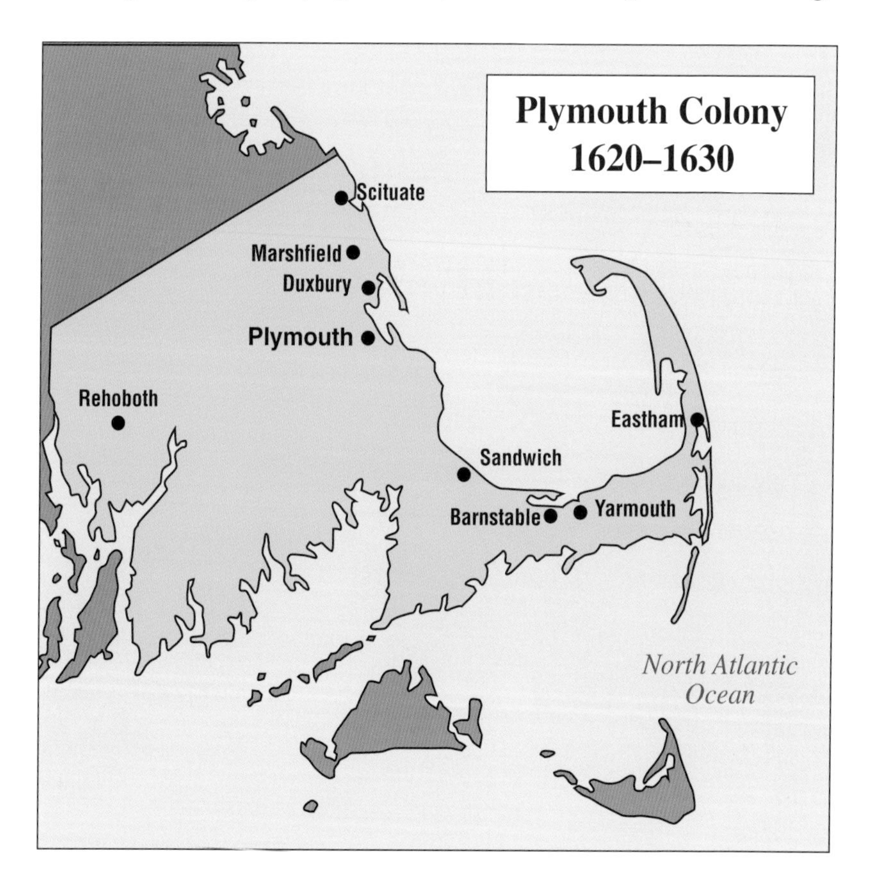

Newly arrived Pilgrims pray during a church service.

another baby was born. The Pilgrims were on their way to a brand new life in the New World.

New Land Sighted

When the Pilgrims first caught sight of the New World, they found nothing but trees and land. There were no houses or stores. No one was there to greet them. The Pilgrims had come to America to find a place all their own and that is exactly what they found. They brought some things with them to help them start.

What the Pilgrims Brought to America

The Pilgrims brought hopes, dreams, and the tools they needed for a new life when they made their voyage to America. They had to bring their own clothes, furniture, bedding, and pots and pans. They brought their European tools and technology. They also brought their Christian faith, and a very English way of doing things. They thought they could re-create an English society in America.

Landing in America

The Pilgrims arrived in America in the fall. Their first task was to build houses so that everyone would have shelter during the coming winter. Each man had to build his own house. Then, together, all of the men pitched in and built the common house, the building in which they could store their supplies. The common house was finished by the middle of January.

It was already too late in the year to plant crops. The Pilgrims would have to rely on hunting and fishing for food. Many Pilgrims suffered from **malnutrition** during the first winter. Others suffered from exposure to the cold winter, and sicknesses, such as pneumonia or tuberculosis. The Pilgrims referred to the illness as "general sickness." Even though about half the Pilgrims who had journeyed to make a new life in America died before the first winter was over, none of the survivors went back to England. Only a few Pilgrims were healthy enough to take care of the sick.

The Pilgrims continued to work very hard to build their new settlement, laying a street with two rows of plots for houses and gardens. Cold, hunger, sickness, and even death were not enough to make the Pilgrims give up and go back to England.

New Neighbors—The Native Americans

The Pilgrims also built a platform with cannons on the top of the hill above their new village. They wanted to

Samoset greets a group of Pilgrims with a friendly welcome.

protect themselves from hostile Indian neighbors. A few months after they arrived in America, the Pilgrims met a Native American, named Samoset, and everything changed. Samoset and a group of other tribesmen came to meet the Pilgrims. Samoset welcomed the Pilgrims to America. Unlike most Native Americans, Samoset knew how to speak some English. He had learned from English fishermen who crossed the North Atlantic every year.

Squanto

Samoset's friend Squanto became the **liaison** between the Pilgrims and the Native Americans. He also spoke English and understood the ways of the Europeans. He had been to Spain and London. When he had returned from England he had found that his family had died in a **plague**. Although originally a Pawtuxet Indian, he later joined the Wampanoag tribe. The Wampanoag were farmers and fishers, and hunters and gatherers.

A Peace Treaty

The Pilgrims realized that their Native American neighbors were kind and helpful people. They no longer worried that Native Americans would hurt them. Squanto and Samoset told their own people that their new neighbors, the Pilgrims, were peaceful and would not hurt the Wampanoag people.

The new neighbors greeted each other kindly and exchanged gifts. Then the Pilgrims, represented by their governor, John Carver, and the Wampanoag, represented by their leader Massasoit, signed a peace treaty. The peace treaty lasted more than fifty years.

Squanto kept communication open between the Pilgrims and the Native Americans.

Lessons from the Native Americans

Squanto became a great friend to the Pilgrims. Although the Pilgrims had brought many things with them when they came to America, they had little knowledge of farming and hunting. In England the Pilgrims had lived in the city, where farming skills were not needed. To help them,

Two Pilgrims stand guard over their families. Despite friendly relations with Native Americans, hostilities did arise from time to time.

Indian corn was one of several crops the Native Americans taught Pilgrims to grow and harvest.

Squanto arranged a meeting between the Pilgrims and Massasoit. Together, Squanto and Massasoit taught the Pilgrims how to find certain kinds of foods, and how to fish for eel, clams, and herring. They taught them to hunt turkey, deer, and bears. In addition, the seeds that the Pilgrims had brought over from England were not growing well in American soil. Squanto showed them how to use fertilizer when planting their crops. This helped the wheat, barley, Indian corn, and peas grow better. The children learned where they could find nuts and edible berries. The Pilgrims believed Squanto had been sent by God to help them. Without the friendship of the Native Americans, it is doubtful any of the Pilgrims would have survived their first winter in America.

A Way of Life

Because the Pilgrims were a religious people, everything they did throughout the day was influenced by the teachings of the Bible and their duty to serve God. They lived pure and simple lives.

Religion—Part of Everyday Life

Religion was such an important part of life for the Pilgrims that they came all the way to America for religious freedom. Not a day went by without prayers. Pilgrims said prayers every morning and every evening. Almost every Pilgrim home had a Bible. The Pilgrims practiced Puritanism and followed a set of rules they believed followed God's prescriptions for life. Dancing, secular singing, and drinking alcohol to excess were not allowed. Other rules told parents how to treat each other and their children, and how to live peacefully in their community.

Going to Church

Every Pilgrim went to church on Sunday. Families walked together to a large area called a **common**. They would meet and greet other families at one end of the common in a building called the **meetinghouse**. The meetinghouse was used as the town hall, as a general social center for the Pilgrims to gather, and as a church. Church leaders and the minister built their own houses close to the meetinghouse.

Church was an all-day event. Puritan ministers gave lengthy sermons. In the winter, it was cold in the meetinghouse. People brought warming boxes filled with hot

Pilgrims make their way to the meetinghouse for their weekly church service.

coals to keep their feet warm. Others brought their dogs to sit on their feet. Children were expected to attend these services and pay attention. Children caught drifting off were tickled by a church official in charge of the tickling rod. Some Pilgrims spent the whole week looking forward to church. Sunday was a day to learn something new, relax, and catch up with friends. It was the one day of the week devoted to rest. For most of their days, however, pilgrims worked hard.

At Home

The Pilgrims' houses were built from logs, and most had dirt floors. A typical Pilgrim home had only one large room. That room was the kitchen, bedroom, and living space. Families who needed a little extra space built a loft.

The homes were very simple, but the families had everything they needed. Along one wall of the house was a fireplace. The fireplace was used not only to keep the house warm, but as the stove and oven, too. The fireplace was also the main source of light within the home.

Along another wall was a set of pegs. At night, the family hung their clothes on these pegs. The men also hung their rifles from these pegs.

Before going to bed, one family member read a passage from the Bible and prayed for the family to stay safe in America. In the beginning, all the Pilgrims slept on the floor. Later they made their own mattresses, and eventually they all had beds. The very young children slept in the trundle beds that slipped out of sight under their parents' beds during the day. Older children, those who were at least seven years old, slept in the loft. Sheets and blankets,

Hard work is put into the construction of a house in Plymouth.

which were stored in a pine chest during the day, were brought out for use at night. On very cold nights, the beds were covered with rugs for extra warmth.

What the Pilgrims Wore

Pilgrims wore simple, durable clothes. Everyone had one basic outfit and another outfit to wear at church and on special occasions. During the week the Pilgrims wore clothes made of bright, cheerful colors. The women and girls wore long woolen dresses and white linen caps that came down over their ears. Men and boys wore long-sleeved shirts, a jacket made of leather or wool, called a **doublet**, pants, called **breeches**, and wool stockings. They covered their heads with knit stocking caps. Boys younger than six years old wore dresses.

On Sundays, the Pilgrims wore somber black and gray. Pilgrim men wore black clothes and tall black hats. The women wore long, gray dresses with a white collar.

Women worked hard to make nice clothes for their families. If there were a rip or a tear in someone's clothes, it was the women's job to stitch it. Because cloth was hard to come by, no clothes were ever thrown away. Old, worn-out clothes were cut into pieces and used as patches for other clothes. Women also sewed blankets and quilts using scraps of material from old clothing.

Everyone Has Work to Do

The more children a family had, the more people there were to help with work. And there was plenty of work to be done. Men worked their farms, fished, and hunted for food. The women took care of the children, prepared the food, cooked the meals, kept the house clean, washed the clothes, and sometimes helped in the fields. Pilgrim children were expected to help their parents around the house and on their family's land. Boys watched the cornfields and protected them from hungry dogs, birds, and wolves. Older boys also helped their fathers build houses. Girls helped their mothers cook, serve meals, wash clothes, and clean house. Children also helped the adults make mattresses. First they would gather dried corn husks, pine needles, or feathers. They would stuff these into linen bags to make mattresses. Children were

A Pilgrim couple, wearing typical clothing of the time, pauses during a walk.

A woman tends to her sewing in this modern-day portrayal of a Pilgrim.

expected to help with other chores as well, such as gathering wood for the fireplace, feeding the chickens, churning butter, fetching water from the well, and helping to serve the family's meals. Children also helped by sweeping floors, grinding fodder for the animals, and tending to the fire, including removing its ashes. Boys spent time working in the fields with their fathers. The children were almost as busy as the adults. There were no televisions and few books and toys to keep the children busy. However, children did make time for one thing that the Pilgrims considered very important: school. Although children did not go to school right away after landing in America, they learned at home. However, because their parents were the teachers, they could teach the children only as much as they themselves knew.

Preparing the Day's Food

Pilgrim women worked hard every day to prepare meals for their families. Cooking was often an all-day task. The children helped out by taking turns cooking a turkey on a spit. This was a hot job because the turkey, attached to a rod, had to be rotated over a fire all day long so that it would cook evenly and not burn. Before eating, the family would first set their table. The houses were small and there was no room to have a large table standing in the middle of the room all the time. The table, two wooden boards placed across sawhorses in the middle of the room, was used only at mealtime.

Adults sat on a bench or on chairs. Children were expected to stand by the table during meals. Mealtime was fairly formal. Children were expected to stay quiet and talk

A woman cooks at a table that is loaded with the types of food Pilgrims ate in the seventeenth century.

only if an adult talked to them first. Everyone kept their hat on during meals. There was little silverware and few plates. A family might have had a few spoons, but most people ate with their hands or used clamshells to scoop their food. Instead of plates, Pilgrims used **trenchers.** A trencher was a piece of wood that was flat on the bottom and hollowed out on the top side to hold food. Because there were not always enough trenchers to go around, the children were expected to share their trenchers.

A modern photograph re-creates a Pilgrim's kitchen as it may have looked.

When mealtime was over, everyone helped clean up. A basket, called a **voider**, was passed around the table. Everyone scraped their crumbs, leftover bones, and napkins into the voider. When the table was cleared off, the boards were taken down and put back up against the wall for the night to make room for the beds. After dinner, the adults would rest. The men and women would relax. The children read books or the Bible. They also played with toys, such as marbles, they had brought with them from England. They also played handball, which people still play today.

Settling In and Spreading Out

Over the next ten years, life in Plymouth Colony changed a great deal. For example, the original system of government changed. When they first arrived, the Pilgrims were governed by John Carver. A year after their arrival, John Carver died suddenly while working in the field. William Bradford took over John Carver's responsibilities as governor. Men and women had to obey the governor, whether they agreed with him or not.

Laws and Voting Rights

It took the Pilgrims more than fifteen years to create their first official book of laws. Another six years passed after that before they had a bill of rights. All along, both men and women were allowed to vote. However, servants, people not considered freemen, were not allowed to vote. However, no law existed that explained who was considered a freeman. Except for the servants, anyone over thirty years old who had a fair amount of wealth and whom the rest of the Pilgrims respected, was usually considered a freeman.

In the years after the Pilgrims arrived in America, more ships came, bringing passengers who would make their home in America. None had it as difficult as the Pilgrims, although most of the new settlers started by building homes in the wilderness, just as the Pilgrims had done. The new settlers were also Puritans, and they docked in the harbor of a village called Boston.

A Road from Here to There

The Pilgrims followed the trails marked by the Native Americans to move about the land. Eventually these trails became their roads. One road ran all the way from Plymouth Colony to Massachusetts Bay Colony in Boston. The Pilgrims needed these roads to make trades with other people. They brought crops and cattle to

A road that was once a trail marked by Native Americans cuts through an area of houses in Plymouth.

A proud Pilgrim looks over the land that gives him and his family food and a home.

Boston and traded or sold them for items they needed in Plymouth or for money.

The Fur Trade

In the first ten years after the Pilgrims settled in America, they set up trading posts in areas that colonists in other parts could easily get to. One of the first trading posts was on Long Island Sound. This trading post was convenient for Pilgrims to trade with the Dutch colony in New Amsterdam, which today is New York. After this trading post, they set up others in Maine and Connecticut. Trading posts were small buildings, similar to stores, where people could come for the purpose of trading their goods for other things they needed. People traded their area's natural resources, such as corn and fish, and especially fur.

One of the most popular furs to trade was beaver fur. Beaver fur could be traded for beads, alcohol, and metals. Trade was carefully regulated. The fur trade was the biggest trade until the middle of the 1630s. By that time, small towns and cities were growing. And, trading posts were abandoned in favor of stores where Pilgrims could get a decent amount of money for their grain and their cattle. The store owners, who were also European settlers themselves, imported goods from Europe. They sold their imported goods to the farmers.

Small Towns

As more and more groups of settlers came to America, they started building small towns that reminded them of the villages where they had lived back in England and in other parts of Europe. For this reason, the entire area came to be known as New England. Although many small towns eventually grew into larger cities, Plymouth itself never became anything larger than a small town. Pilgrims gave their towns beautiful names such as Longmeadow and Springfield. As the towns grew, so did the number of buildings. Perhaps the most important of the buildings was the general store. There, women could buy fabric to make clothes, men could purchase tools, and children might pick out a small piece of candy. At the mills, powered by the town's stream, wheat was ground into flour and wood was sawed into pieces. Before long the candle maker, the furniture maker, and the blacksmith all had shops of their own. Some of the bigger towns even had inns in which travelers could stay. Almost every town had a school.

The small village of Boston grew into a thriving New England town by the 1660s.

The Children Go to School

Pilgrim children got a year off from school after they landed in America to help their families get settled. But once the houses were built and everyone was settled in, the children went back to school. Teaching children was so important that the Pilgrims passed laws to enforce it.

Children of different ages listen to their instructor in a one-room classroom in Plymouth.

The clock tower of Harvard University, the first college established by the Pilgrims.

One law stated that children must learn to read. Another stated that every town that had more than fifty families had to have a schoolteacher. The law even said that all the people living in the town, not just the families who had children, had to pay the teacher. The Pilgrims set up the first public school system.

Colleges

It was not long after the Pilgrims arrived in America that they opened their first college. That college is still well known today. It is called Harvard University. Students

A member of the Pilgrim militia protects his territory from an attack.

came from nearby Virginia and from as far away as England to study at Harvard. Why would students travel all the way from England just to go to college? In England, Puritans were not allowed to go to college. If they wanted to study, they had to move away.

Defending Their Territory

Although the Pilgrims had long since made peace and become friendly with their Native American neighbors, they still feared attack. Other settlers who later came to America from Spain, France, and Holland all posed some threat to the Pilgrims. It was not uncommon for fights to break out between these groups. To defend themselves, the Pilgrims organized a **militia.** All the men under the age of sixty were required to undergo training. In the event of an attack, they would know how to defend their territory. Boys joined the militia when they turned sixteen. The militia had regular drills, or practices, so that the men could keep their skills sharp. Every household was required to have a large gun for protection.

Life for the Pilgrims was not easy. But their strength, determination, courage, and religious beliefs helped them succeed in America where they turned stark wilderness into beautiful towns and cities.

Glossary

breeches: Short pants fastening below the knee.

common: A large grassy area used by Pilgrims.

doublet: A close-fitting jacket worn by men especially in the sixteenth and seventeenth centuries.

hold: The part of the ship below the deck in which cargo is stored.

indentured servants: Servants owing time to someone in exchange for money, or in this case, passage to America.

liaison: A person who acts as a go-between.

malnutrition: A condition in which a person is not fed well enough to stay healthy.

meetinghouse: A building of the common used on Sundays as church, as the town hall, and as a general social center for the Pilgrims.

militia: A group of citizens who have some military training, and who are called to service only in emergencies.

plague: A disease that infects many people in a small area, leaving many people dead.

trenchers: A piece of wood, flat on the bottom and hollowed out on the top side to hold food.

voider: A basket passed around the table after a meal into which everyone scraped their crumbs, leftover bones, and napkins.

For Further Exploration

James Daugherty, *The Landing of the Pilgrims*. New York: Landmark Books, 1978. This historic book for young readers is not only informative, but also fun to read. It is presented in story form with illustrations.

Joy Hakim, *A History of Us: The First Americans*. New York: Oxford Press, 1999. This book is one of an eleven-book History of the United States series. It is full of period illustrations, timelines and dates, key historical figures, geography, social attitudes, contemporary concerns and dilemmas, and political climate and trivia. Sidebars raise questions to challenge analysis of how the facts presented relate to various aspects of history.

———, *A History of Us: From Colonies to Country*. New York: Oxford Press, 1999. This book is also in the eleven-book History of the United States series.

———, *A History of Us: Making Thirteen Colonies*. New York: Oxford Press, 1999. This is a third book in the History of the United States series.

Anne Kamma, *If You Were At . . . The First Thanksgiving*. New York: Scholastic, 2001. Each illustrated page asks and answers a new question about the Pilgrims' first Thanksgiving.

David C. King, *Colonial Days: Discover the Past with Fun Projects, Games, Activities, and Recipes*. New York: John Wiley & Sons, 1998. Learn all about the Pilgrims with these hands-on, fun-to-do projects. Each project is illustrated and fully explained for hours of learning and fun.

Ann McGovern, *If You . . . Sailed on the Mayflower in 1620*. New York: Scholastic, 1993. Page-by-page lively question-and-answer style, this fact-filled book answers all sorts of questions about the Pilgrims' journey on the *Mayflower* and their first year in America.

Kate Waters, *Giving Thanks: The 1621 Harvest Feast*. New York: Scholastic, 2001. A photographic reenactment, based on true historical accounts of what might have taken place in the fall of 1621 between the Pilgrims and the Wampanoag at the first Thanksgiving.

Index

Picture Credits

On cover: © Pilgrim Society, Pilgrim Hall Museum
© Corel Corporation, 39
© Catherine Karnow/CORBIS, 28
Brandy Noon, 12
© North Wind Pictures, 7, 9, 10, 11, 13, 16, 18, 19, 20, 23, 25, 27, 34, 35, 37, 38, 40
© Richard T. Nowitz/CORBIS, 30
© Lee Snider/CORBIS, 31

About the Author

Melanie Ann Apel holds a bachelor's degree in theater arts from Bradley University and a bachelor's degree in respiratory care from National-Louis University. Melanie has written more than thirty nonfiction books for children and young adults. This is her first book for KidHaven Press. When she is not writing, Melanie loves to read, figure skate, and spend time with friends and family, especially her beautiful baby boy. Melanie and her husband and son live in Chicago.